Book of Prayers

J. M. R. Larman

Copyright © Jessie Larman 2019
First Edition: ISBN - 0958540748
Second Edition Carnarvon Art Studio 2019

All rights reserved. This book is copyright. Apart from any fair dealing for the purpose of private study, research, criticism or review, as permitted under the Copyright Act, no part of this book may be reproduced or transmitted in any form or by any means, electronic or mechanical, including photocopying, recording or by any information storage and retrieval systems without written permission from the publisher. Enquiries should be made to the publisher.

Cover Photograph: J. Larman.

National Library of Australia

A catalogue record for this book is available from the National Library of Australia

ISBN: 9780987207548 (paperback)
Distributed in Australia and Overseas by IngramSpark

✝

For God so loved the world, that He gave His only begotten Son, that whosoever believeth in Him should not perish but have everlasting life.

John: Chapter 3 verse 16.

Jesus is Lord

God Bless You Today

....

Whether you are a new or mature Christian,
I pray that God will bless you as you use,
read and pray from this book.

If you are not sure how to pray, I hope this book
will be of help to you.
However, if you already are used to praying
maybe you will be encouraged afresh by some
of the prayers that are here.

...

Written & Illustrated by: Jessie M.R. Larman.
©
Carnarvon Art Studio
P.O. Box. 149
Carnarvon.
Western .Australia 6701.

E-mail: j.larman@wn.com.au

I.S.B.N. Number...0 9585407 4 8

✝

Acknowledgements:

*Special thanks and blessings
for helping to edit this book
go to
our daughter Ruth.*

*Also
Thank you and God Bless
to all
who have helped this Book come to Fruition.*

Scripture quotations taken from the Holy Bible,
New International Version.
Copyright © 1973, 1978, 1984
by International Bible Society.
Plus Old King James version of the Bible.

Jesus is Lord

John Chapter: 15 verse 5

*I am the Vine; you are the Branches.
If a man remains in me and I in him, he will bear much
fruit, apart from me you can do nothing.*

Prayer is Powerful

Never Underestimate the Power of Prayer.

Jesus Is Lord

Lord of all the Earth
Lord of all Creation.

He Is My Lord
Is He Your Lord?

He Reigns on High in Heaven
Angels Bow Down Before Him
& Praise Him Forever More

He is The Lord
He is God's Only Son
And He Is Alive.

INTRODUCTION

My Testimony

This is to let you know that The Lord Jesus Christ
Healed my lungs of an incurable disease
in 1984 in Perth, Western Australia by the
laying on of hands at a Church
Service there.
Praise The Lord for His Healing Power
The same now as when Jesus walked upon the earth.
Also I have come to know The Holy Spirit
More fully in my life
Since inviting Him into my body
So that the Lord God can use me
For His work and Glory.
The Holy Spirit is our Teacher,
Comforter also our Guide.
He wants us to fellowship with Him each day.
He is the one who helps us to pray.
His presence is lovely,
Once you have lived with The Holy Spirit
(who is The Spirit of Jesus Christ)
You will never want to live without Him.
...

Book of Prayers

✡

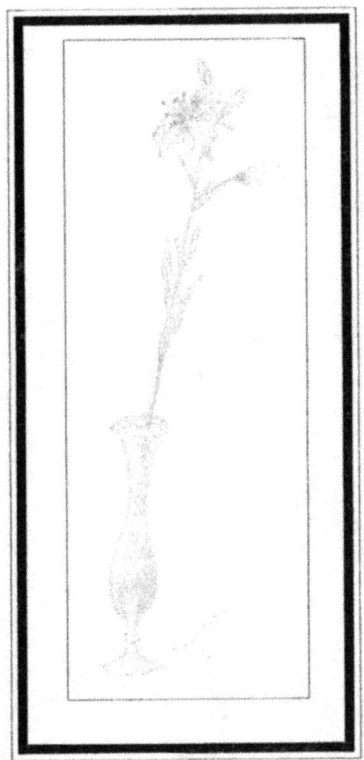

A Help You To Pray Book.

Bible Verse: Regarding Praying.
1 Thessalonians: Chapter 5 verse 17 says:- Pray without Ceasing.

Jesus is Lord

*I sought The Lord and He heard me
and delivered me from all my fears.
Psalm: 34 verse 4*

Every Day Prayers

For

Every Day People.

Jesus is Lord

Here in this book is a selection of Prayers to pray for different occasions and personal prayers that will help open the doorway into the Throne room of God.

...

God, Almighty God is our Heavenly Father; we know this because of the Prayer that Jesus taught His Disciples.

It is a prayer that can be prayed daily called:

The Lord's Prayer

which can be found in the Bible.

(in the New Testament)

St. Luke: Chapter 11 verse 2.
also in
St. Matthew: Chapter 6 verse 9.

...

Here is a version of The Lords Prayer.

Most versions differ from each other but the meaning is always the same, this is the way that I particularly like to pray this Prayer.

From <u>St. Luke: Chapter 11 verse 2</u>
in your Holy Bible.

...

Our Father who art in Heaven,
Hallowed be your Name.
Your Kingdom come.
Your Will be Done.
On Earth as it is in Heaven
Give us today our daily bread.
And Forgive us our Trespasses, as
We Forgive those who sin against us.
Lead us not into Temptation
But Deliver us from evil.
For Yours is the Kingdom,
The Power and The Glory,
For Ever and Ever - Amen.

...

The Lords Prayer is very special it covers everything we need to pray for.

Jesus is Lord

1st.   We acknowledge our Father in Heaven:

*Our Father who art in Heaven
Hallowed be Thy Name.*

We are telling Him that we love His Name – it is hallowed (holy). He is our Heavenly Father, our Spiritual Father, very different from our earthly Father. He loves us very much and wants us all on earth to be part of His family. When we accept Jesus into our lives then we are part of God's family, Jesus being God's only begotten Son then becomes our brother by adoption as well as our Saviour. God is very jealous of his children and sends His Angels to guard us. We need to show respect and love to (our Father who art in Heaven) to respect His holy Name….
YAHWEH The LORD

…

2nd.   Let us acknowledge His Kingdom in Heaven:

*Your Kingdom come,
Your will be done,
On earth as it is in Heaven.*

We ask for His Kingdom to come and for His will to be done on earth as it is in Heaven.
We are aware in this Prayer, that Jesus is letting us know that there is a place called Heaven where things are surely done in a most holy way.
Heaven must be very beautiful with God in charge, Jesus at His right hand and The Holy Spirit there as well.

Myriads of Angels are worshipping God.

Everything is pure and light. There is no darkness in Heaven, nor any sin; nothing unholy can be there.

In The Lord's Prayer we are asking that this can be so on earth, that the people on earth can be free from sin.
We need to pray and mean this for ourselves as individuals, for our families, friends and for the world.

...

3rd. Then it goes on to say:

'Give us today our daily bread'

This does not just mean bread to eat, it means everything that we need to be able to live on this earth, food, clothing, shelter, love, peace, joy.
Especially I believe it means The Word of God, which we need to read daily from the Bible because that is food, bread, for our own spirit and soul. Therefore we need to eat and digest The Word of God.

...

4th. Next we have:

'Forgive us our Trespasses
As we forgive those who trespass against us.'

We ask in The Lord's Prayer that He forgives us our trespasses as we forgive those that trespass against us.
This truly is awesome, we will not go into the great depth of it in this book but you may like to consider what it really means. God will show you more of the meaning if you ask Him.
However, the bottom line is the fact that if someone hurts us in

anyway and we do not forgive them, even though we are in the right and have done nothing wrong to that person in thought, word or deed then we are not forgiven for the incident either.

God forgives us as we forgive.

Sometimes we find that if we hold unforgiveness in our hearts it can manifest as a sickness in us - sometimes it could be arthritis for instance, when we realize regarding the fact that we hold unforgiveness in our hearts and then pray, repent and forgive the person whom we hold a grudge against and really mean it, the words that Jesus said on the cross - 'Father forgive them for they know not what they do' Luke Chapter: 23 verse 34, our Father in Heaven then allows Jesus to forgive and heal us.

(As we have forgiven them).

Think for a moment: is there anyone who you know that you need to forgive. If so right now, if you feel like it you can talk to God and ask Him to help you to forgive them. It may only take a minute or two but you must really mean it when you say (I forgive - so and so - for what they said or did against me, at such and such a time, I release them to you God and do not hold a grudge against them anymore) Please forgive me God for taking so long to say that I forgive them, cleanse me from the sin of unforgiveness, so that I can walk better with The Lord Jesus. Thank you that you bless me now and take away the hurt that I felt when they came against me as they did. I know that I am not supposed to judge, that you are our judge Lord and that you say you will judge us as we judge others. Thank you for listening to me, blessing me and helping me to overcome the feeling of rejection that was with me by not forgiving the person who I have just forgiven Lord God.   Amen.

> *'Father forgive them
> for they know not what they do'*

...

5th.

*'Lead us not into temptation
but deliver us from evil.'*

Well what about that then? How often are we tempted each day and how hard it is to resist sometimes.
Some people have the excuse that the devil made them do it! That is a nonsense because we have been given free will to choose!
We can say yes or no, you can do it (whatever it is) or not do it. The devil of course can tempt us each day, as he tempted Jesus in the desert.
Remember what Jesus said in the Bible in St. Matthew: Chapter 4 verse 10   "Away from me, Satan! For it is written; 'Worship The Lord your God and serve Him only.'"

So you see even Jesus was tempted.

However He shows us the way to deal with temptation i.e. to resist the devil and he will flee away from us.
In other words we do not have to do those wrong things day after day.
If we do wrong and we truly are sorry, then we must repent, ask Jesus to forgive us and He will. He wants us to repent, as He truly wants to forgive us our sins.
Remember though, that to repent is not the same as saying

'sorry' - yes we need to say sorry but actually to repent and ask for forgiveness is the place we come to when we are so sorry for what we have done in thought, word or deed that we never ever want to say or do that wrong thing again.

When we pray with our whole heart and are truly sorry for our misdeeds, in that repentance you can feel the forgiveness of Jesus flow through and cleanse you. Then you know in your heart that you will never be tempted by that thing again, whatever it was. Praise The Lord that He has mercy on us as we must have mercy on those who come against us.

You see when we sin we come against God and He has feelings too. So He feels the hurt like we feel when someone hurts us, that's why we need to repent and tell Him we are sorry when we have done wrong.

He does not punish us for the wrong - He forgives us and rejoices that we have realized we made a mistake and want to alter our ways of living.

...

6th.   What about this statement then?

> *'For Yours is the Kingdom,*
> *The Power and The Glory,*
> *For Ever and Ever - Amen.'*

This means that God's is the Kingdom, the Power and The Glory for eternity. No one else, He is Almighty God, full of Power and Glory and He lives forever. He lives in our Prayers and Praises and shows His Power in many ways throughout the earth. Also His Glory He shows in numerous ways. Part of His Glory and Power are shown by the miraculous healings and His Grace allowing us to come into Salvation.

...

What better way can we pray than the way that Jesus has shown us!
I believe it is a great privilege to pray and receive wonderful answers to our prayers.

Jesus is Lord

To Pray Really Effective Prayers.

Well to do that we must of course have invited Jesus into our hearts, into our lives. Because it says in the Bible - the way to the Father is through The Son.

<u>St. John: 14 v 6.</u>

Jesus said,
"I am the way and the truth and the life. No one comes to The Father except through me"

...

Prayer is Powerful…

Jesus says in <u>St. John: 14 v 13 - 14</u>

"And I will do what ever you ask in my name, so that The Son may bring Glory to The Father. You may ask me for anything in my name and I will do it"

This is a promise from Jesus.

...

> And I tell you, ask and it will be given you;
> seek and you will find;
> knock and it will be opened to you.
> Luke: Chapter 11 verse 9

A Place to Pray.

In Church we can pray of course but to pray at home is different, here are some suggestions to get you started if you are not used to praying much at home.

First: Choose a Time.

(You need to be on your own)

It must be a time that suits you, either first thing in the morning is good, before you go to bed at night or maybe after lunch. If things are new to you, ten minutes will be enough to start with for a while, then gradually you will find that the time goes and maybe half an hour or more has gone by. As you get used to sitting with God even an hour will not seem long enough sometimes.

Second: Find a Place:

Where you decide to sit and pray is very important for praying each day. It needs to be somewhere where you are going to be comfortable, maybe a favourite chair in the lounge-room or sitting in bed before you sleep or even in bed before getting up. The main thing is to try to keep to much the same time and place each day - it's like making an appointment with God. After a few days you will look forward to your appointment with God. He will be there waiting for you to begin.

Jesus is Lord

Third: What to do?

Well now you have a time and place in your mind, what are you actually going to do or pray for:
Here are a few suggestions to get you started if all this is unfamiliar to you.

Things you will need:
most important of course will be a good Bible, that you are going to be happy with. Some of the really modern versions are not for me, I really like the Old King James. However for normal Bible reading the New King James is excellent, also I like the N.I.V. (New International Version)
Spend a bit of time selecting one that will suit yourself, it may seem a bit expensive but will last you for many years and will be a blessing to you.
Also you will need a note pad and pencil, this is to write things down when you think God is saying something special to you, or you may like to write a few special words of what you are reading down, so that you can remember them and refer to them later.

Now, you may ask how am I supposed to know what to read and how will God talk to me?
Well, what I have found and have suggested this to others is to start at the beginning of the Bible in Genesis: verse 1...either read a whole Chapter or even only half a page, then put a pencil mark in the margin when you have finished reading, ready to

carry on from that place the next day. Sometimes it is best to read only a small portion then re-read that part to receive more understanding of it before moving on. Likewise in the <u>same prayer time</u> beginning at the start of the New Testament Matthew: Chapter 1 verse 1 do the same thing.

Ask The Holy Spirit to begin to show you what it all means as you read.

After your readings you may like to do likewise with the Psalms, or leave them until another time.

Something else - very important I believe is to make a cuppa or take a glass of water to put beside you so there will be no need to excuse yourself and interrupt your prayer time to get up and find a drink.

The idea is to be comfortable and begin to enjoy sitting there at the feet of Jesus. (That's what some people call their prayer time).

Prayer Time:

Now, when you eventually get to sit down for your Prayer Time and Reading....First of all Pray and submit yourself to God, ask Jesus to forgive you for any wrong things you have done, also try to forgive anyone whom you know that you have not forgiven, ask Jesus to help you to do this, then ask the Holy Spirit to be with you and guide you and help you with your Prayers and Reading.

When you get used to sitting with God you will find that in between the readings you can pray, if you are not sure what or how to pray, just start talking to God as you would to me or to a special friend. What ever is on your mind concerning your family or friends, church, town, neighbours, animals, pets, house, finance, holidays, health, even housework, anything at all, talk to God and ask His help and advice - (that is prayer) -

(Talking to God is Prayer.)

We do not always have to ask Him for things. A lovely thing to do is to Praise Him and thank Him for all your Blessings. Thank God for your family, your house, your belongings, your friends, your food, your clothes, anything special that comes to mind in your Prayer Time to be glad about. Remember that it is a gift from God, so thank Him as you would an earthly Father.

If you are blessed with speaking in tongues (that's Gods Heavenly Language that The Holy Spirit speaks through our tongue directly to God our Heavenly Father) it is then something really special to allow him to help us pray.

Remember when Jesus went up to Heaven he said He would not leave us on our own but would send His Holy Spirit to be with us.

Well He did, remember in the Bible it say's He came at Pentecost.

> Acts: Chapter 2 verse 4.
> All of them were filled with The Holy Spirit
> and began to speak in other tongues
> as The Spirit enabled them.

> That I believe it was the beginning of the Church
> as we know it today.

So you can begin to see that a Prayer time can certainly not be boring. When you first start of course five or six minutes may be all that you can manage but as you continue each day you will find more things to pray about and your Bible Readings will begin to be more interesting when you understand better what you are reading.

If you get stuck, you could sit and read part of a Christian book during the special time that you have set aside.

Also nowadays there are quite a few Personal Bible Studies - you could possibly embark on one of those.

A good thing to do is to go along to a Bible Study now and again at your local Church. If they do not have one you can study with a friend. There are lots of ways to learn about Jesus and our Heavenly Father and the Kingdom of God.

As you continue to do any of these things, The Lord will bless you.

Talking about being blessed do you know that each day you can ask God to Bless you?

Ask Him to Bless you and make you stronger in your Spirit, Soul, Mind and Body and He will.

You see God has given us free will and it must be lovely for Him to see us use that free will to ask Him to Bless us.

He say's ask of me and you shall receive. Imagine all the Blessings we miss out on because we do not ask!

We like to go our own way most of the time thinking we know what is best and are so clever, we even forget to thank Him for our Blessings.

Remember how sad you have been when you have done something special for someone and they haven't even said 'thank you'?

Well our Heavenly Father has feelings too.

Really we are very fortunate because through Jesus we truly have a Hot Line to God!

Having a prayer line straight to God we can quite easily say thank you to God any time, anywhere.

Really there must be many people who do not know that we can truly ask God to bless us.

We need Him to bless us so that we can be a blessing to others.

Likewise if we are in any kind of trouble or upset we can use our own personal Hot Line to ask Jesus for help. Our Hot Line is through The Holy Spirit, through Jesus to God our Heavenly Father.

There is a very quick prayer - the quickest one ever, it is - 'God Help' - and He is there.

There are lots of different ways to be comfortable when we pray, for instance we can sit, stand or kneel. We can pray on the bus, plane, in the car, walking, running, playing, swimming - almost anywhere and especially lying on our bed.

The possibilities are endless, even in one day there are twenty-four hours in which to pray. Surely we can set aside even ten minutes to be with God!

Do you know that the twenty-four hours of the day can be divided up as follows - eight hours work, eight hours play, eight hours sleep. We can choose how to break those up to suit ourselves but the work and play should be to the Glory of God for The Kingdom of God.

One thing I have found is that exercise and good sensible food must be included in the work and play time.

We have been given our bodies but when we accept Jesus into our heart then our body belongs to Him. Our body then is a temple (a dwelling place) for The Holy Spirit.

We are asked in the Bible to keep our bodies Holy unto The Lord. That means physically and spiritually clean. That is another area to pray about.

Pray for God to (bless the food that we eat) as whatever goes into our bodies has an effect concerning our health. There could be another book on that subject alone, so we will not go any further with that now apart from saying that it is definitely a good prayer point to put on our list of things to pray for.

If you are not already a Christian,
here is a Prayer for you to pray to become one.

TO BE A CHRISTIAN

Dear Jesus I know I am a sinner I repent of my sins, please forgive me and come in to my heart to take charge of my life.
Thank you.
You are now Lord of my life,
I also acknowledge God as Father and accept your Holy Spirit……Amen.

…

If you pray the above Prayer and really mean it you are immediately accepted by Jesus. You are Born Again and belong to the Kingdom of God. You need to tell a Christian that you have taken this step, to speak out is an action of faith and confirms that you have now become a Christian.

You need to begin reading the Bible.
St. John: Chapter 3 verse 3. Says:
Jesus declared, "I tell you the truth, no-one can see the Kingdom of God unless he is born again."

…

(May God Bless You With His Love.)

Please read through a couple of times to make sure you can pray it with your heart and really mean it before you make your commitment to God.

Jesus is Lord

Your life in Jesus will truly begin when you exercise your faith and tell someone what you have done.
Tell them that you have invited Jesus into your life, into your heart.
You will begin to feel different, you won't want to swear or use Jesus name wrongly as so many people do.
It will begin to grieve your spirit when you hear the name of Jesus being defiled.
If possible please speak out to let people know that you do not approve of them taking The Lord's name in vain.
One thing you can say, when they use Jesus name as a swear word is that He can hear them.
Or maybe say Jesus is pleased when you call out to Him.
It will stop them in their tracks, make them think what they are saying.
If we condone them using the Lord's Name as a swear word then we are as guilty as they are by not speaking out against what they are saying.

Jesus name is above all names, He is Lord, the King of Kings, God's own true Son. He came to earth especially for our sakes, died on the cross for our sins. We should always honour His name (Jesus)

Jesus is the only way to The Father.

We can only pray acceptable effective prayers when we know Jesus as Lord of our lives.
When we are part of God's Kingdom, as one of His children He listens and waits for our Prayers day by day.
Prayers are POWERFUL when they are prayed in accordance with Gods will and directly from our heart.

Prayer accomplishes things that we never can.
Never underestimate the Power of Prayer.

Here is a Prayer that I especially like:

Prayer

Dear God I pray that I may be filled
With Righteousness that comes through your
Son Jesus Christ. (Philippians Chapter 1 verse 11)
I pray that Jesus may be Lord of my life
For ever and ever.

May I grow in your love God and be
Filled evermore with your Holy Spirit,
Also with your fruits and gifts of The Holy Spirit.
That you may use me to help others,
I pray that I may be so filled with your love,
Peace and joy that it may emanate through me
For others to see.

That they may come to know Jesus,
That He died for us on the cross.
I pray that my sins are forgiven,
please God and help me to know when
You have forgiven me each time.—Please God,
So that I can feel that release in my Spirit
To do your will each day and forever.

I pray that I never forget or take for granted
That Jesus died for my sins on the cross,
That only through Him am I saved.
Giving you my body for your Holy Spirit
To work through and use as a temple for you God.
May I ever know your saving grace
And live in your Kingdom forever.
Amen.

Jesus is Lord

If there is anything special that you need to ask God for today, just continue to pray asking God our Heavenly Father for what comes to mind. Talk to God about your special needs and fears, ask for His help if you need it today. However big or trivial, He wants you to ask and talk to Him about it.

Learn to sit and talk to our Heavenly Father and if at any time you are distressed about anything ask Him to allow The Holy Spirit to comfort you.
When Jesus went to Heaven, remember He said that He would leave His Holy Spirit here on earth to comfort and fellowship with us. But we do need to ask, God loves us to seek His face and bring all things before Him.

Do you know that you can talk to The Holy Spirit day and night, He is with us forever as long as we want Him to be. It is a great comfort to know that wherever we go or whatever we do The Holy Spirit is with us. We are never alone, once we have invited Jesus into our lives. Remember Jesus died for us on the cross and He intercedes at God's right hand for us. Jesus Loves us, He died especially for us (you and me) on the Cross and His Blood has washed us clean.

There is so much to learn about Prayer and the only way to learn is to practice each day.
It's wonderful when you actually see the answers to your prayers come into being.
Then you can truly Praise God and thank Him for that special thing that He has done that you have been praying for.

> Jesus said:
> ..."Let the little Children come to Me and do not hinder them, for the Kingdom of God belongs to such as these...
> Mark: 10 v 14.

Suggestions that may help you to Pray.

In the following pages are some suggestions
that you can use as prayers,
or use to help you to get started
to pray in your own way
to God for the things
that are on your heart
in your own special prayer time.

...

*This is the day the Lord has made.
We will rejoice and be glad in it.
Psalm 118 verse 24.*

Jesus is Lord

*Angels are all around us,
helping us each day.*

✞

To Pray for our Families is most important.
(Exodus: 20 verse 12.)

Here is a prayer you may like to use sometimes. Just alter it around to suit your way of praying, also do likewise with all the other prayers in this book.

Remember:-
(Families that Pray together, are more likely to stay together.)
...
Ask The Holy Spirit to help you to Pray. Then begin..............

Dear God I pray especially today for my family and friends. Here you may like to name some of the members of your own family i.e. (Husband, Wife, Children, Parents, Grandparents, Grandchildren also anyone else who is included in your family that you would like to pray for today.)
I pray Lord God that you will bless all my family, especially those that I have named before you today. I pray that those who don't know the Lord Jesus will soon come to the knowledge and love of Him. I pray that you will bless my family with your love and blessings today of peace, joy, contentment, good food and finance also may we have good friends.
Also especially, I pray for the health of all members of my family God that they may receive your wonderful healing in their spirit, soul, mind and body today wherever they need it most.
Thank you God for all your wonderful blessings for us all. Thank you that you have blessed me with my earthly family, please may I be a blessing to all of them today and forever. Thank you for your Angels guarding us and our individual Guardian Angels that are with us.
I praise you Lord God through Jesus Christ my Lord and Saviour.

Amen.

Jesus is Lord

Let us Pray for Ourselves.

We need to pray for ourselves. You will find that one prayer sometimes leads to another and that you will eventually not need this book, or any other as you come before God each day in prayer.

Here then is a prayer for Ourselves. (My self) (Yourself)

This is for the start of the day, just alter the words to suit afternoon or evening.

Ask The Holy Spirit to help you to Pray. Then begin...............

Dear God I come to you through Jesus Christ my Lord, I praise your Holy Name and pray that you would kindly Bless me today. Thank you Heavenly Father for keeping me through the night and keep me through this day.
Dear Lord Jesus I repent of my sins, please forgive me and help me to forgive myself. I thank you that you have forgiven me.
May I walk with your Holy Spirit today and He with me, in truth, love, peace, joy, grace, comfort and contentment please.
Use me for your praise and glory God, organize my day, bring before me those who you want to bring here today and let your love and peace be with us.
Would you fill this house and property Heavenly Father with the love of Jesus. Please allow your Angels to guard this house and property, including myself.
Thank you God for my guardian Angel, I believe He must be very beautiful. I thank you for all your blessings towards me God. Jesus thank you that you allow your Holy Spirit to be with me now and forever.   Amen.

James: 5 verse 16

The Effectual Fervent Prayer of a Righteous Man Availeth Much.

Jesus is Lord

A Prayer for Animals
(Genesis: 1 verses 20 - 25.)

A Short Prayer could be:

I pray for all animals throughout the world that they may be beautiful for you Lord. Please bless them with food and shelter today.

Amen.

...

If you would like to pray a longer prayer it could go something like this if you feel like talking to God for a bit longer:-

Animals are so beautiful Lord, they give us so much pleasure, creatures large and small are part of your creation. I thank you that you made them all. The domesticated ones are mostly so soft and gentle like the cats and dogs with their beautiful kittens and puppies. We appreciate the giant size creatures - Elephants, Giraffes and all the other wild creatures throughout the world.
How can we ever give you enough thanks and praise Lord God for every creature that you have made?
It's so wonderful that you have provided special food and shelter for all creatures upon this earth.
Thank you also that you allow us to have animals as pets. They are so special Lord.
I pray that no-one hurts your creatures today. Please heal any that need healing and may good homes be found for those that need them, thank you God. Amen.

A Prayer for the Government.

I would like to thank you for our Government God.

Would you Bless them all today who are working in the Government of this Country please, so that they may Govern righteously and truthfully each day.

May our Parliamentarians come to know Jesus as Lord of their lives so that eventually we could possibly have a truly Christian Government.

I pray for good health for our Government workers, especially for the Prime Minister, for your divine protection of him as he travels around the world promoting good relationships towards this Country.

Lord I pray for all people in authority, every government Dept., throughout the world for their thoughts and actions to be righteous especially now in this world today with all it's problems.

Please bless all Government workers and heads of State, Prime Ministers, Governor Generals and Ambassadors in every Country throughout world, keep them safe in your care.

Let them remember that people are precious and that they are working for us not just for themselves and their friends, that we need to be governed with propriety and in the love of The Lord Jesus.

Let us not judge them too harshly when they make mistakes making laws that we are not in agreement with. We know that you will judge them God when the time comes for some of the outrageous laws that have been passed that are not in agreement with your word in the Bible. May wrong laws be rescinded and the correct ones put in their place. Give the members of Parliament boldness to vote with a clear conscience on future debates and laws that will be right for governing our Country.

Amen.

Jesus is Lord

Prayer for those Studying.

Today Lord God I would like to pray for all those who are studying.
Young children, adolescents also men and women as they work through their respective studies. Those who are taking exams today please guide them to remember the correct answers if indeed they have put in the time required to understand the work that they have been learning.
Dear God please bless all the children starting out on the first years of Schooling, may their learning be a pleasure to them—not a burden so that they can enjoy their school years.
For Adults who are restudying to enter the workforce, please guide them in their chosen career.
Especially I pray for everyone young and old who are studying your Word today in the Bible Lord. Please bless them with peace and joy in their hearts as your mysteries are revealed to them.
May your Holy Spirit guide and help them with their learning.
Also thank you that you continue to help me in my studying and learning as I go on with my Christian Walk.

I ask these things through Jesus Christ my Lord.
Amen.

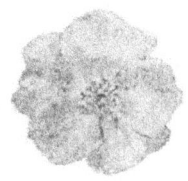

Pray for Lost Souls.

I know that your heart grieves God for all those lost souls who have not come to the knowledge and love of Jesus yet.

I pray Lord God that you will allow your Holy Spirit to move around them to somehow soften their hard hearts towards you.

I pray today that Christians will be able to speak out of the love of Jesus so that those who are not saved will indeed begin to wonder what they are missing out on.

I pray that today many souls will come into Salvation through out the world.

Help us as Christians to reach out to those who are in the world, help us to reach out with love, joy and peace to who-ever you bring before us today.

May your signs and miracles continue through out the world as a sure witness that Jesus is alive, that He lives for ever and ever with you God Our Father in Heaven.

Bless all who come before us today God and also please bless me so that I too can be a blessing for others.

Amen.

Jesus is Lord

Prayer for Retired People

Dear Lord God our Heavenly Father I ask a blessing now for all Retired people. Having worked all their working life for wages may they enjoy their new found freedom of not having to get up and clock in for work each day.

May their retirement years be a source of blessing for them and for their families. Perhaps a time for some to see more of their grandchildren and their own children of course.

For some may it be a lovely time of togetherness if they are married.

Others might be ready for a new adventure of travel, or getting involved in special hobbies that could have taken a back seat for many years.

Some in their retirement may like to be involved with voluntary work - there always seems to be a need - especially in our Church family in various ways.

Please let those who have retired not feel rejected or unwanted, may they come to know Jesus in their lives if they do not already know Him. It would be a real blessing to themselves and to the world if every retiree could come into Salvation and walk in the Love of The Lord Jesus.   Amen.

✝

To Pray for those who are ill (Sick)

Dear Lord,

for everyone who is ill today in any way whatsoever please could they receive some of your divine healing.

We know that with time you allow some things to heal themselves like cuts and bruises, cough's and cold's.

But Lord God there are so many on this earth who are dying of incurable diseases, please have mercy on them.

Send your Christians to lay hands on the sick, you say in the Bible (Mark Chapter 16 verse 18 ...Lay hands on the sick and they shall recover). Or bring the sick to Christians who You have anointed especially to pray for the sick. Help us who are Christians to be obedient to do your will when you ask us to pray for who-ever You bring to us.

We know that truly Jesus is our healer dear God, that through the blood of Jesus we can be made whole in our spirit, soul, mind and body.

I pray Lord God that you will allow Jesus to continue to heal me day by day in my spirit, soul, mind and body so that I can be a blessing to others that you bring before me each day. Also God, I pray that I may be a blessing to my family please. Thank You God.   Amen.

Jesus is Lord

Prayer for Poorer Countries

It's so sad God when we see pictures on the television and in the Newspapers of people in the poorer Countries of the world.

I pray today that everyone would be able to have something to eat, also shelter against the elements. I pray that special aid that is transported from us more affluent countries goes directly to the people that it is intended for and is not filtered off before it arrives. I pray for your Angels God to guard each assignment including the couriers and people involved.

For those in the poorer countries may they begin to receive more help from around the world, including extra goods and finance.

I pray that the Governments of the underdeveloped countries begin to be filled with Christians who will see that the aid is delivered fairly and honestly.

I pray that children will be able to go to school and participate in the development of their country as they grow in knowledge and wisdom. Amen.

A Prayer for all Artists, Authors, Musicians, Actors, Actresses, Dancers, etc..

Dear Lord God I pray for all to whom you have given these lovely gifts to be Artists, Authors, Musicians, Actors, Actresses, Dancers etc., I pray for everyone who is involved with any craft work that it may be worthy and pleasing to you. For all of us who are Christians I pray that our work in any of these gifts will be a help to your Kingdom here on earth.

May our art and craft be a pleasure to us as we use the many talents and gifts that you have kindly bestowed on us. Lord help us to help others when ever we can. Let us be a blessing to teach the young ones the best way we know how, so that they in their turn can produce beautiful works for you God and for Jesus with your Holy Spirit's help who is in us and with us.

Thank you God for the special talents that you allow me to have. I am very grateful to you.
    Please show me the best way to use the gifts
        that you have given me.
           Amen.

Jesus is Lord

Prayer for the Media, T.V. & Radio.

Well Lord God this is a difficult Prayer to pray for the Media, Television & Radio because they are so influential in the lives of everyone here in this world. I pray that you will continue to use these avenues for your praise and glory more and more in the coming years for evangelizing and spreading the Gospel of Jesus Christ my Lord to the ends of the earth. So that everyone who hears will want to become saved - into your Kingdom God on earth and out of the Worldly Kingdom. I praise you that you allow us to have the Media which of course involves all Literature, Newspapers, Books etc., and that soon maybe the ungodly things in all of these will begin to take a back seat so that your Kingdom will rule.

In Jesus name I pray this prayer Lord God.

I know that in some parts of the world your Word is going out mightily and that many people are being saved, I pray for protection for all involved in these industries of the different kinds of Media. That your Angels guard them as they continue to fight the good fight for the Gospel to be Preached throughout the world as you have commissioned us to do in the Bible. Amen.

...

Matthew: 24 v 14.
And this gospel of the Kingdom will be preached in the whole world as a testimony to all nations and then the end will come.

✞

To Pray for Creation.

Creation is wonderful God, you made it and you looked at it and saw that 'it was very good'.

(Genesis Chapter 1 verse 31.)

Dear Lord God it is good, I am grateful for the grass, the trees, the sea, the air we breathe. Thank you for the amazing sunsets that you create as if painting a new picture each day. The morning sunrise, the spectacular views of valleys, mountains and plains. Every flower is so special so beautiful, each with its perfect shape and perfume, each plant and tree you have fashioned differently. The great strong Oaks and mighty Palms to the tiniest blades of grass. Who could ever doubt you God when they see your wonderful creation of this earth. We stand in awe at the incredible waterfalls, listening to them thunder nonstop over the cliffs and mountain ranges. You have fashioned the large expanse of Rain Forests, Oceans, Seas, Rivers and Streams. You have brought them all to life with myriads of underwater, plants, seaweed, coral and all living flora. Your creation of this earth is incredible, marvellous, spectacular, we praise you Lord God and know that you are The Almighty, Ever Living God of Creation. Amen.

Jesus is Lord

Pray for Abandoned and Aborted Babies.

Lord God it is so sad that some babies are not wanted. I know babies are so precious to you, you make them and yet people cannot comprehend the terrible things they do in aborting them and abandoning them.

Babies are so beautiful God, such lovely little souls, incapable of looking after themselves even for a moment. Please have mercy on all who have intentionally aborted or abandoned their babies. Bless all the babies who's souls have gone from this earth Lord. I pray that you are happy to receive them in Heaven.

For those who truly repent of the terrible act of getting rid of their babies please forgive them, for spiritually they know not what they do or have done.

Those that are truly remorseful grant them your peace.

May the abandoned babies be found good Christian homes if possible God so that they too can come to know Jesus as Lord of their lives.

Amen.

✝

Prayer for Doctors & Nurses.

Heavenly Father thank you that you have given us Doctors and Nurses. We know that through them you have given authority and power to use the various medications regarding healing for us.

We do know that you can sovereignly heal but also that you have given us Doctors and Nurses to care for the sick, injured and dying. Please grant them grace and the love of The Lord Jesus to minister to all who come before them. Allow them to work with confidence and compassion, kindness and gentleness. We thank you God for Surgeons, Midwives, Doctors in private practice and in our hospitals. For all Doctors and Nurses throughout the world we give you praise and thanks. Bless them who work long hours and those in the worn torn countries. Please grant them the expertise that they need, the facilities and the medications necessary to dispense for their patients.

Amen.

...

We praise you Lord God that St. Luke was a Physician, so we do know that you have used Doctors through the ages. Also thank you that Florence Nightingale initiated the need for Nurses during her lifetime (1820 - 1910)

Jesus is Lord

Let us pray for the Weather.

The weather is most important to us here on earth God. We certainly need the sun the wind and the rain. I pray for all places today where they need rain that you would allow it to fall - especially over the drought stricken areas Lord, the farms the Sheep and Cattle Stations, Plantations and all places involved with producing crops and livestock.

We are so blessed here in Australia with the wonderful sunshine and warmth that it gives and the breezes and winds that you send to cool us Lord.

It's wonderful to see the deserts come alive after the rains.

We cannot fully comprehend the Seasons but we appreciate them Heavenly Father.

The snow falls on the mountains and the land looks beautiful, pure white as white can be...a Winter Wonderland.

All around the world the weather is so different from place to place.

Thank you that you have ordained the weather as it should be, thank you that you hear our prayers especially when we need rain or sun.

Please hear our prayers when we call out to you for any special needs regarding the weather.

Thank You Lord   Amen.

✝

Let us Pray for those in Hospital.

May all those in Hospital today God receive special care. Please can the right diagnosis be found so that the Doctors can prescribe the correct medication.
Let the Doctors and Nurses be truly dedicated to their work and to the patients.
Please would you allow Christians to visit and encourage their friends and loved ones, in the Word of The Lord who are in Hospital today.
Have mercy on all who are in Hospital God, let your healing hand be upon them. Also for those who call on the name of Jesus may they truly receive some of your Divine healing.
You are our healer Lord and we know that you can heal through the medication given through the Doctors and the care given through the Nurses as well as by your Sovereign Divine Miraculous healing. So I ask that you Bless all of those who are in hospital today Lord with peace and faith in their hearts for their particular needs. Ease their pain, heal their wounds, take away their suffering and make them whole.
Help us as Christians to pray in our hearts silently for healing, when ever we visit any patients in hospital. Maybe out loud if they would like us to, so that they can know the love of The Lord Jesus more in their lives.   Amen.

Jesus is Lord

Let us Pray for Refugees

Lord God I really don't know how best to pray for Refugees except to ask that you bless them in some way today.
Those who find they would rather go back to their original Country please could you make a way for them to do so.
Grant patience to Refugees in all Countries while they wait to find their more permanent homes.
I pray that all Refugees may have food, clothing and shelter today and that you would continue to protect them all, especially the children please God.
All in charge of Refugees, grant them to have compassion so that they treat all in their care with respect and decency.
I pray that whoever are Christians in the Refugee Camps will be able to minister to their companions whilst awaiting their residency.
Thank you Heavenly Father that you hear my Prayers.

Amen.

A Prayer for those Newly Married.

When people are first married God it is such a special time. The love they have for each other is so precious, they hope and pray that it will last a life time.

For some people Lord this truly does happen but for others it is sad that it doesn't.

I pray today that who-ever are making their marriage vows that they will be able to uphold them and be faithful to each other as you have ordained that we should be in the Bible.

I pray that you will bless all people being married today whether they are young or older and also those who are being married for a second time.

May they be able to share the love of The Lord Jesus with each other in their lives and try to live Godly happy lives with your Presence God in their hearts and homes.

                            Amen.

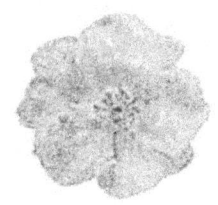

Jesus is Lord

To Pray for those in the Air.

To some of us Lord God it seems miraculous that planes can fly, how they can defy gravity and are able to cruise through the clouds so high in the sky.

I pray that you could keep all Aircraft safe to-day, that you would bless the pilots with commonsense and discernment, also expertise to maneuver their particular aircraft safely today. May your Angels guard all those who are flying today and may they take off and land safely at their chosen destination.

As seats are chosen and allocated to people before they board the planes, could you organize the seating so that you can place Christians in the right seats to talk or minister to those sitting beside them.

May your Holy Spirit guide them in their speaking so that today souls can be saved even in the air.   Amen.

☩

To Pray for those on the Ocean's and Sea's.

You have made the Ocean wide and deep, a vast expanse of water God.
Please bless and keep safe all who sail on the ocean to-day. The big ships, the smaller vessels, all who go out in boats today, keep them safe Lord, especially any who are in storms at sea or who's vessels are not properly sea worthy.
Grant them wisdom to know what to do in an emergency, please allow your Angels to guard them.
Also those who are swimming and surfing, fishing or just playing in the ocean along the beautiful beaches. Keep them safe from predators, like sharks, stinging jelly fish and strong undercurrents that come in with the tide, grant your Angels guard over them.
For all who work and play in or on the ocean, may they appreciate the wonders that you have placed in and around the oceans and seas of this earth.
Thank you Lord God for the beauty of the ocean and seas displaying the marvellous reflections of light at sunrise and sunset.   Amen.

Jesus is Lord

Let us pray for our Country.

This is our Country, this is our land, dear God it is beautiful, most parts too beautiful to describe.

We have wonderful landscapes, oceans, a vast expanse of sky. Most beautiful creatures you have given us in our Country to love and cherish, to look at and appreciate.

Giant Whales in the ocean, tiny sea creatures and all the land animals, wild and tame.

This is our Country and I praise you Heavenly Father that you allow us to live, work and play here.

Help us to look after this country in the right way.

I pray that you will bless this land with sun and rain for producing the crops to feed the population of people here also all the abundance of animals and sea creatures in this Country and throughout the world.

May your peace reign with us here, may many come into Salvation today dear God throughout this land.

Amen.

For those who are Unfinancial.

It's so dreadful God to not be financial, by that I mean to have no money available even for the necessities of our day to day living. I pray for those without work to be able to earn wages, that positions be found for them especially those who have families to support.

Some of us know what it is like to count every cent and to go without things that others take for granted.

Please help all who are struggling today to make ends meet, that they may be blessed with gifts of food or finance - what ever their needs are today because of lack of money please help them God. It's so lovely when extra finance comes along.

I pray Heavenly Father that you will continue to open the windows of Heaven for finance for me and my family please today and I thank you that you have and I pray that you will continue to do so forever and ever.

Thank you God. Amen.

Jesus is Lord

A Prayer for those who are Travelling.

So many people are travelling around these days God, in planes, cars, boats, ships, all sorts of transport including buses, trains, bicycles, motorbikes. We truly are able to travel the world in this day and age more than ever before. But Lord God I pray for your help to keep us safe while we are travelling on the land, sea or in the air. Please allow your Angels to guard us including me and my family especially today as we go about our travels, also as we go back and forth to work or just visiting family and friends.

I ask for your protection God as I myself drive the car to go shopping.

Lord God I know that you like us to ask for your protection where ever we go, so I ask especially for you to be with us all throughout the world as we travel on any form of transport not just today but always. Thank you Lord God that you protect the Drivers, Pilots, Captains and all who are in charge of any type of vehicle today so that the passengers will be delivered safely to their destinations.

Thank you Heavenly Father.   Amen.

A Prayer for the Clergy

What a privilege dear God for anyone to be a Clergyman, a Minister, or a Priest in your Service. Thank you Heavenly Father that you choose these people to work for you in your Church.

We do know that you are not so concerned with Church denominations but that you are concerned with the hearts of men.

I pray that those called into your service do not abuse their positions and that they will minister with your Holy Spirit anointing upon them more and more in the days and years to come. Please bless them God to listen and hear your voice, not the voice of the people. Bring them to their knees in repentance for any wrong thoughts or deeds, so that they can minister in faith, truth and righteousness, your Holy Word from the Bible to their respective Churches who you have entrusted to their care.

Amen.

Jesus is Lord

Pray for those in Nursing Homes for the Aged.

Dear God, so many people now are in Nursing Homes for the Aged. Lots of families think it best that their Parents and Grandparents have special care in Nursing Homes that they themselves cannot provide for them in their own homes. Please grant the elderly peace in their hearts today as many of them await their new life in Heaven.

Allow your Holy Spirit to comfort them, help and enable them to come into Salvation before they depart from this world. Help their families to visit more frequently, don't let them just leave them in Nursing Homes or Homes for the Aged and forget they are still part of the family. For those without anyone to visit them, whose families are far away or that they have none, please bless them with special friends to talk to and share in their lives each day.

Take away the loneliness from the hearts of all aged people in Nursing homes Lord, fill them with the peace and the love of Jesus. Also I pray for those who care for them that they will have compassion, so that they can treat the elderly with the dignity and respect that they are entitled to, knowing that one day they may indeed be in their place.

Amen.

Intercessory Prayer

To Intercede for someone or something special is to pray with all your heart and soul and with all your being - then let The Holy Spirit take over when you cannot find the words to pray.

Give the whole prayer to God our Heavenly Father the best way that you can and leave it with Him to organize the outcome of your Prayer.

Never doubt that God can do more than we ask with our Prayers.

This can be a very tiring exercise and you need to be on your own knowing that there will be no interruptions with family or friends around.

This is truly where you get in your prayer closet as some people call it, come into that special place with Jesus and pray until you can pray for that person or thing no longer, you will know when the prayer is finished. Then having done all, we stand.........that is - we wait on God.....we must get on with our daily lives knowing that He is working on our behalf.

Jesus is Lord

Index
List of Prayers:

Prayer for:	Page No.
Abandoned & Aborted Babies	44
Artists, Authors etc.,	41
Animals	34
Clergy	55
Creation	43
Doctors & Nurses	45
Government	35
Families	31
Homes for the Aged	56
Hospital Patients	47
Intercessory Prayer	57
Lost Souls	37
Media, T.V. & Radio	42
Newly Married	49
On the Oceans & Seas	51
Our Country	52
Ourselves	32
Poorer Countries	40
Refugees	48
Retired People	38
(Sick) Those who are ill	39
Studying	36
Those in the Air	50
Travelling	54
Unfinancial	53
Weather	46

✝

"This is the day that

the LORD

hath made:

we will rejoice and be glad in

it."

Psalm: 118 v 24

Jesus is Lord

The Author Jessie Larman was born in England. She married in 1958, emigrated to Australia in 1973 with her Husband and their three young children.
A Naturalized Australian Citizen she is fortunate to have at this present time (year 2003) eleven Grandchildren.
Was healed of an incurable disease in 1984 in Perth, Western Australia. Jessie at the moment is living in Carnarvon, North West Australia where she has her Art Studio, being involved with Desktop Publishing, Oil Painting etc.,.

✟

*In Prayer Let Your Soul Soar
as on the wings of
an Eagle.*

Jesus is Lord

Harry.

*Thank You Lord that you Bless
Our
Families
&
Pets.*

✝

Updated Edition, 2019

Printed in Australia

Jesus is Lord

Praise God

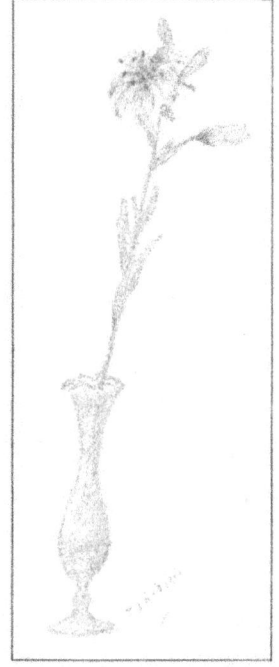

Jesus is Lord

I.S.B.N Number...0 9585407 4 8

Jesus is Lord.
Lord of the Ocean & Lord of the Seas.
Lord of the Land & Lord of the Skies.

Soar into the Heavenly Realms
Like an Eagle on wings of Prayer.

www.ingramcontent.com/pod-product-compliance
Lightning Source LLC
Chambersburg PA
CBHW050607300426
44112CB00013B/2109